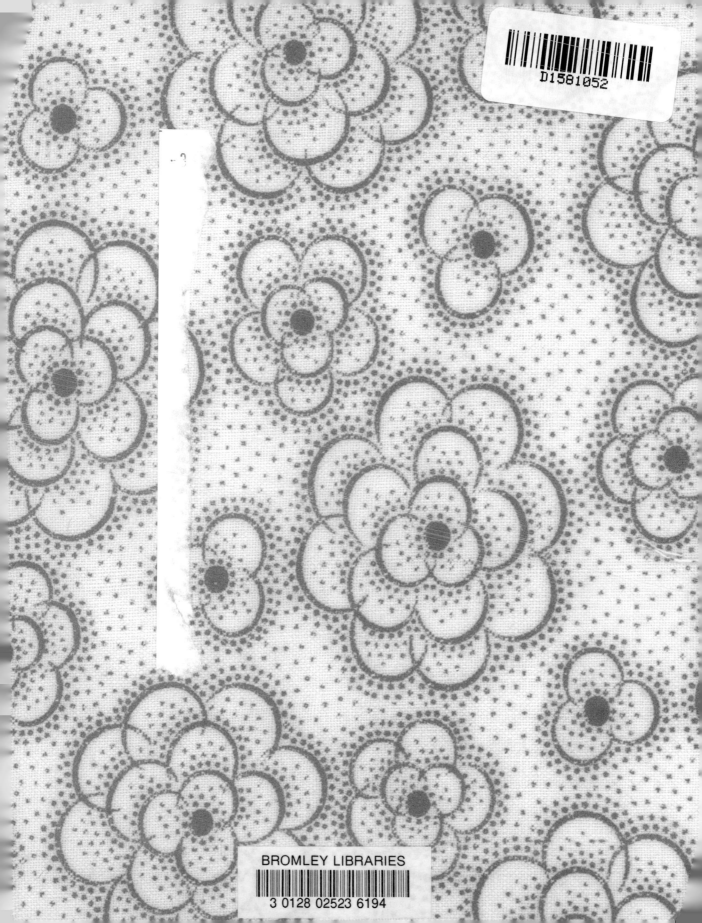

Cath Kidston® in print

Photography by Pia Tryde

Quadrille

contents

introduction

Ever since I was a small child, I've had an intense fascination for print. Although my memory is terrible for many things, such as telephone numbers, I can recall every print throughout our house as I was growing up: the striped rose bedroom curtains, the magnolia print in our playroom, the lilacs in the spare bedroom, and so on. The same goes for clothing: my favourite strawberry-print sundress, the rainbow-coloured stripes on my sand shoes and, of course, my first psychedelic trouser suit.

I began buying vintage prints as a teenager, when it was popular to trawl flea markets for 'Granny' dresses. It was also a time when many great contemporary fashion designers were in their heyday – Laura Ashley, Celia Birtwell for Ossie Clarke and, of course, Biba and Kenzo. Sadly, I neglected to save anything from that time, but each of these designers have proved to be hugely influential over the years.

As I became involved in interior design, I began to seriously collect vintage fabric. I have an enormous respect for all things original, so reusing an old pair of curtains, rather than buying something new, appealed to me. Alongside the interior decorating, I started a business dealing in old fabrics and found there were some great vintage prints around. In the early nineties, the taste in interiors was for ornate, overblown 'country house' decoration, which has never appealed to me. I prefer a much fresher look, still using these great old floral prints but placing them in a much cleaner, more contemporary setting. The concept for my present business was born.

In my first shop, I sold colourful painted furniture and lots of second-hand fabrics. I had a vision of white-washed walls, freshly painted furniture and cheery cabbage rose fabrics with minimum fuss and frills. Inspired by my childhood nursery – with its gloss-painted pale pink walls, lino floor and oversized chintz chair covers – I sought to reinvent this look for a modern space. I like things that have a practical, utilitarian feel to them, so the idea of a floral-print ironing board cover, a plastic-coated table cloth and even a shopping bag appeals much more than designing any amount of heavy swags, tails and festoon blinds. I began to take vintage documents and re-work them into what I saw as contemporary floral prints in new, fresh colourways and with bolder layouts.

Once I began selling ironing board covers, the business really took off and the fun began thinking up a range of products for the store. Now we sell over 500 items around the world, from dog beds to bath towels, hair ties to handbags. I still collect old prints – it is a compulsion I am sure will never leave me – and the fabrics provide me with new ideas each season.

I hope this book provides inspiration to others, just as seeking out and working with wonderful old prints stimulates me. As I am hopeless at sewing, many of the ideas included here are very simple, be it cutting up brushed cotton pyjamas into dusters or covering a brick with funky retro florals to use as a doorstop. If you are lucky enough to be able to sew, the possibilities really are endless, and if not, there are always people who can help. As far as I am concerned, my main enjoyment is in inventing endless ideas for using print – often with surprising and impressive end results!

big florals

big florals, for me, are the epitome of a classic print. A huge bunch of roses or a combination of cottage garden flowers, such as hollyhocks and delphiniums, set against a white or washed-out background colour immediately springs to mind. But there is a very fine line between these sort of prints looking rather sad and gloomy and having a wonderfully cheery effect, which is nearly always down to colour. It doesn't matter how old the fabrics are or what variety of flowers they depict, just as long as the palette has a freshness to it. Anything too muted and autumnal will look dull, while even the most traditional flower design in great colours can look really contemporary.

Vintage prints from the 1930s and earlier are some of the best, with beautifully hand-painted flowers in vibrant colours. Because of their age, they tend to be fragile and are therefore hard to find. Many of my favourite prints are colourful designs from the fifties, such as classic roses, and if you are lucky, you can still find reasonably large pieces. There are plenty of oversized floral prints available today, often copies of archive designs. I am often disappointed by how few have that winning combination of colour and print to really work, but there are some good ones to be found. When you buy new fabric, it can be worth washing it down to give it more character or sometimes even running a pale-coloured dye through it. Washed blues, green and pinks often succeed in giving a fabric a fifties feel.

Uncluttered rooms are where I prefer to use big floral prints, in quite a simple way, rather than mixing them with other patterns. I loathed the 'country house' look of the eighties, when rooms were smothered in print and felt really claustrophobic. If a design is strong enough, it will stand out well in a room on its own. Curtains made up in an oversized floral print can sometimes look too traditional, whereas a chair cover made in such a fabric always seems to work. A simple tablecloth looks good in a big floral, as does a single splash of print used for a bedhead or bedcover. It is also fun to make something unexpected, such as a beanbag, in a really traditional floral fabric.

Remnants and small lengths of big floral prints can be used up in all sorts of ways. A pair of bold printed pillowcases look great contrasted with white bedlinen. Card lampshades are easy to recover with fabric: straight drum shades work well as they have a modern style to them. Even a single bunch from a flower design stretched over a frame can make a perfect picture.

bean bags

bean bags are incredibly comfortable, which is why I like them so much, but all too often they are covered in garish prints. I found this bean bag in our attic, left over from our child's playroom, and recovered it with a piece of old-fashioned French chintz. It has replaced an armchair in our spare bedroom, where it has added an element of fun in what was quite a serious looking room as well as offering our guests a quiet place to relax. By recovering an existing bean bag, I kept the sewing to a minimum: this way you can slip the new cover over the old bean bag and not have to worry about making an additional lining. Some bean bags are made from a simple round top and bottom, joined by a straight panel. Others, like the cover shown here, are made from a single piece of fabric that is sewn into a tube and then stitched with six or so large darts at either end to form a point. Either way, the bean bag is sewn with simple seams (see page 157). When sewing the last seam, however, you must remember to leave a large opening to either slip the new cover over the existing bean bag or fill it with beads. As bean bags often get dragged across floors, I would recommend using a reasonably hardwearing fabric, such as linen, to withstand any wear and tear.

13

seat cushions

can revive tired armchairs, giving a new lease of life with a fresh splash of print. The feather cushion on this chair was worn out, but rather than re-cover the whole thing, I replaced just a single cushion and then had an extra scatter cushion covered in the leftover fabric. The same could be done to a worn-out sofa, perhaps even using different prints for each seat cushion to create an excellent patchwork effect. For more complex upholstery jobs, I use a professional seamstress, but if you are relatively competent sewer then you might want to tackle a simple shaped seat cushion yourself (see page 157). Don't forget that if you only have just enough fabric for the top and front edge of the seat cushion, you can always make up the underside and back with another fabric in a plain colour.

garden kneelers are not

often great looking. I bought mine, with its original basic plaid top and waterproof base, from my local garden centre. To give it a facelift, I hand-stitched some floral-print cotton over the top of the plaid; it is just so much easier to customise an existing kneeler than make one from scratch. Cut your chosen fabric to the size of the top, turn and press a hem to the wrong side on each side and then neatly sew in place by hand (see page 157). I have used a bright white sewing thread to contrast with the deep reds and greens of the floral print. A bright fabric, such as a printed corduroy, would be perfect; look out for old skirts in junk shops. A keen gardener would love this for a gift, wrapped with a pair of gardening gloves or a book.

pretty aprons

were almost obligatory in the fifties; something to show off over an outfit while you served dinner. There are some amazing vintage pinnies, with crazy prints, lacy trims and all sorts of pockets, frills and other details, to be found in second-hand shops. If nothing else, they look great hanging on the back of the kitchen door. To make your own, decide whether you prefer a retro waist-tie pinny or a classic cook's apron, like the one shown here. I often keep it simple and use lengths of cotton tape for the waist ties, instead of making them. To finish, add one or two practical patch pockets (see page 157).

PURE IRISH LINEN

19

tablecloths

are the perfect way to show off those big, bold floral designs that were so popular in the fifties, especially if laid over long refectory tables or used outdoors, where they can really make an impact. It's fun to accentuate any unexpected mixes of colours by teaming a tablecloth with mismatched napkins in primary colours or pastel, ice-cream shades and, just to add to the riot of colour, seat your guests on a selection of vivid gloss-painted chairs. A plain tablecloth is the easiest project to sew if you're a beginner; stitch simple hems along all sides of a piece of fabric cut to size (see page 158). That's it! It doesn't even matter too much if your seams aren't perfectly straight, it only adds a little homespun charm.

24

delicate chintzes

are a little impractical, but they are irresistibly pretty and often cheap to pick up. This small piece of floral chintz cotton fitted perfectly into an old picture frame that I found at a car boot sale, but it would look equally good under glass as a bedside tabletop, where it wouldn't suffer any wear and tear. I often find decorative picture frames in dark woods, but they can be transformed easily with a couple of layers of pale chalky paint and a top coat of wax polish.

fifties florals

make delightful loose covers for bedrooms. I inherited this very tall, shaped bedhead, which I recovered in this striking, oversized rose print. To keep everything in proportion, the bed itself is raised on a wooden platform: not only does this create excellent storage space underneath, it also gives the bed a rather grand, stately look. Apart from a couple of printed silk scatter cushions, the covered bedhead provides the only pattern in the room; I deliberately left the walls a plain pale turquoise as a counterpoint to the vibrant red and yellow rose print. Here, it was important to choose a bold floral as a more muted print might have looked rather old fashioned. I have piped the seams on the front of the cover shown here (see page 158), which can be a little tricky when sewing around curves. Just take your time and carefully tack all the seams before stitching for a neat finish.

laundry bags

in basic white cotton or linen can be given added interest with appliqué flowers cut from scraps of print (see page 157). This is really easy to do. Once you have cut around the flowers, lay them on the bag and either pin or tack in place. Alternatively, stick them down with a light squirt of photographic spraymount. This will hold the appliqué in place perfectly while you sew it to the bag using small, neat slip stitches. I left the edge of this appliqué raw and used a matching colour sewing thread, but you could also hem the patch or use a different colour thread for contrast, providing your sewing is really neat.

bedrooms, such as

this studio room, can be simple spaces with little else but a mattress or futon thrown on the floor. I love the fact that these two different prints are the only form of decoration in this all-white bedroom. The combination of retro spots and classic cabbage roses lends this room a warm, friendly feeling, despite its apparent emptiness. Teaming spots and florals in an otherwise white space lends a contemporary edge to the prints, while the fabrics help to soften an uncompromisingly modern room.

lampshades are the

perfect way to use up any small scraps of a favourite
fabric, as you need only a tiny amount to wrap around a
frame that can then be stitched in place (see page 158).
With this pair of bedroom lamps, I have indulged
myself by adding gay feather butterflies to the frilly
shades, but I make sure that they are kept well away
from the lightbulbs so as not to be a fire hazard.

practical bedcovers

are essential for any pet owner, as muddy paw prints are so often a problem. In our household, my dog, Stanley, has a habit of dashing upstairs after his night-time walk and diving straight on the bed. A 'blanket cover' that gets washed every week is the answer. I have a huge selection of prints I use in our bedroom, but this large piece of unlined chintz is a favourite. There is no need to line the cover – leaving it unlined makes it easier to launder – so just stitch it with simple hems (see page 157). Depending on the size of your bed, join two or more widths of fabric, taking care to match up the print, until the cover is the width required. Look out for patterned flat sheets that you can also use in this way – the ultimate no-sew bedcover.

lined drawers
are rare these days, as many people can't be bothered with the fuss, but the joy I gain from using this immaculately lined cupboard is tremendous. I had only a couple of rolls of this hand-blocked rose-print wallpaper, so rather than paste it on a wall, I paid someone to professionally line a cherished chest of drawers. Even if you simply pin down some wallpaper or giftwrap with drawing pins, it is well worth doing.

practical prints

practical prints are some of my favourite fabrics—oilcloth, sticky-backed fabric, towelling — despite being made for specifically utilitarian, rather than decorative, purposes. While lengths of vintage fabrics are quite hard to find, there are numerous sources of new practical fabrics, providing you know where to look. The fun is in thinking of alternative ways of using them.

Towelling printed in stripes or florals is always worth looking out for. There is a wide selection around; large department stores are a good place to look. Striped beach towels make an ideal pair of bathroom curtains, or look equally great in a kitchen or laundry. I recently made a loose cover for an armchair from some spotty towelling, which works particularly well in a kid's room. Street markets are always my first stop when I am on holiday. I have found some great cheap towels in Italy and Spain, such as an enormous rose print, which I made into giant towelling cushions. They are ideal for lounging outdoors or in a conservatory, but also make great floor cushions. Unusual flannels are also worth collecting. I keep a pile of them, all in different prints, in a big bowl in our bathroom, and they look great all together.

Oilcloth is another of my favourite fabrics; its glossy coating gives any print a modern twist. Its traditional use is for tablecloths, but it is an ideal upholstery fabric. Prosaic kitchen chairs and stools can be transformed with shiny seat cushions, but it is also fun to use oilcloth on grander pieces of furniture. I recently covered a pair of nineteenth-century French bedroom chairs in rosy oilcloth. If you are re-covering antique furniture, I recommend getting it done professionally. My upholsterer covered our chairs immaculately, finishing the edges with traditional brass nails. I have also made an instant tabletop by covering a piece of chipboard in oilcloth using a staple gun. Set atop a basic trestle base painted in white gloss, this is a great way to make cheap tables for a party. It's fun to use a different print for each table.

Old-fashioned hardware stores are a good place to rummage around for sticky-backed fabric in wonderful patterns. You may find some basic check and marbled prints, or even some retro kitchen-utensil designs or florals. Their traditional use is for drawer lining, but a great print stuck over a tabletop not only looks good but wears well. Leftover scraps are ideal for covering cookbooks. Most of these old-fashioned, utilitarian fabrics are really cheap to buy, but the effects can be startling when they are used well.

wipe-clean tabletops

can be easily created using self-adhesive plastic-coated fabric, which is not only excellent for lining kitchen drawers, but makes a pretty work surface, too. Sticky-back plastic is still very popular in Europe, so I often pick up a few rolls from hardware stores when I am on holiday. You can find some great old-fashioned vegetable prints and florals, as well as the ever-popular gingham checks. When sticking the fabric down, work across the table from one side to the other. Personally, I don't worry about any wrinkles, but if you want a perfectly smooth surface, ease out any air bubbles as you go, because they can form creases that are hard to remove later on. Once the sticky-back plastic is stuck down, trim off any surplus.

upholstered steps, painted
in white gloss and given an oilcloth top in one of my own modern floral prints, have found a home in my bathroom. This robust, hardworking fabric can be put to all sorts of uses besides tablecloths: I have used oilcloth to reupholster kitchen stools, chairs and even worn-out car seats (see page 158). The high-gloss coating on the fabric really brings out the colours of a print, giving it a modern edge.

43

funky flannels, made from

pure cotton printed with unusual diagonal stripes in strong shades, are irresistible. I buy them in bulk in as many colours as possible. I love the combination of all these bright cotton flannels, so I pile them up together in a dish in my bathroom.

pop-print towels

can be made from retro towelling curtains with just the minimum of sewing (see page 158), just as bathroom curtains can be made from a pair of bath sheets. As much as I love a completely plain bathroom, I cannot resist using printed towelling. It's fun to layer pattern upon pattern: I team this loud seventies floral with a more traditional rose-print hand towel, which I picked up in a street market, and my own spot fabric. Seventies pop-print designs are hard to find in any great quantity, but if you are lucky enough to get hold of a reasonable length, they make the most perfect loose covers for bathroom chairs. Nowadays, you can find some great contemporary designs that take on a new light once transformed into curtains or upholstery.

47

bathrooms come in all shapes and sizes;
I am lucky to have a large enough room to hold a free-standing cast-iron
bath that sits underneath a large window. I prefer to keep fixtures and

fittings in bathrooms white, and introduce colour and pattern with the old
hint of printed fabric. Towelling is the natural choice for a bathroom,
because of its high absorbency, and comes in a huge range of colours and
patterns. Another trick, is to trim white towels with a favourite ribbon.

tea towels

are ideal projects for beginner sewers to practise their skills on the sewing machine. Any old cotton or linen fabric will do, cut to size and stitched with a basic straight hem. Add a hanging loop made from ribbon or sew a tie from any leftover fabric (see page 158). Homemade tea towels, tied with raffia or ribbon, make an ideal 'granny gift'.

dusters

are my latest obsession! I prefer to recycle fabrics whenever possible, so any suitable scraps of printed brushed cotton, even old pyjamas, I cut into squares and reuse in a flash. This pink pictoral print is far too garish to be made into children's clothing, but it is absolutely ideal for the cleaning bucket. Dusters are the fabulous no-sew project as you don't even have to stitch any hems; simply cut the fabric with pinking shears to create a zigzag edge or leave them frayed, as I have done here.

gift boxes

are a great way of utilising otherwise strange prints. This dogtooth check with roses was really rather ugly as a large piece, but cut down into small scraps and glued in place to cover matchboxes, it comes into its own. A bundle of covered matchboxes tied up in an acetate bag make an excellent cheap gift, or use the box as packaging for tiny precious presents, such as a pair of earrings or a brooch. If you are covering a matchbox, remember to leave the strike strip uncovered.

drum lampshades

, for some reason, are excellent when covered with a more unusual print. I had this material in a drawer for years and was never quite sure what to do with it. But when I needed a shade for this bright yellow lampbase, it really came into its own. It is easy to cover a basic drum shade with non-flammable spray glue, so long as you cut the fabric to the exact size (see page 157). Add only the smallest amount for a hem, as if you fold over too deep a hem it will show through when the light is switched on.

abstract prints

are still easy to pick up and well worth looking out for, despite the fact that they are becoming increasingly fashionable. There are famous designs by artists such as Lucienne Day, which are expensive and collectable. They tend to appear at better auction houses and are a serious investment, not to be chopped into cushions. Because I know little about this era, I am always cautious about cutting fabric up for cushions without looking at the seams. Fabrics are normally named along the edge if they are by a famous studio or artist, so it really is worth checking before you get out the scissors. Then there are the more everyday graphic designs from the fifties and sixties, which have been made into curtains and chair covers, that I come across in charity shops and car boot sales. These are worth snapping up.

Framed fabrics can look terrific. A large piece of print in the right colours, stretched over a canvas frame, makes a wonderful picture. Likewise, some of these vintage designs in unusual colour combinations would look hideous furnishing today's homes, but they can work really well for fashion. Recently, I bought a piece that was black with khaki and lime green squares that I made into a really chic tote bag. The same goes for satin upholstery prints from the fifties in geometric designs, which make up into great evening bags. If you see an interesting print but are not sure what to do with it, snap it up as an idea will always come along later.

Graphic florals, particularly those from the seventies, are coming back in yet they are still cheap to pick up. Look out for swirly flowers in psychedelic colours at charity shops and car boot sales. Internet auction sites are a good hunting ground for this kind of thing, but do check what kind of fabric you are buying. Polycotton is best avoided, but it was quite common in this era, particularly for duvet covers and curtains.

Used sparingly, a little print goes a long way. One of my favourite projects in this book is the doorstop on page 67, covered in a funky floral linen. I recently looked through some old seventies decorating books; the prints were hideously overpowering as curtains and wallpapers. That said, I recently took a pop print from my own collection and had it painted onto my caravan. It caused quite a stir on its way to the Glastonbury Festival. I guess there is something about these big, bold prints out in the open air that simply brings a smile to the face!

wall hangings

made from framed abstract textile designs make wonderful pictures. Although this style of print has become very sought after, the odd retro print can occasionally turn up in thrift shops. This yellow 'atomic' print was originally made up into a pair of typical fifties short curtains. As these designs are becoming very collectable, it is best not to chop them up too much but to hang one entire curtain as a painting, stretching the fabric like a canvas over a wooden frame (see page 158). You can buy ready-made stretchers from art shops, but these only come in standard sizes. Otherwise, you can go to a picture framer who will make a stretcher to order, tailor-made to fit the piece of fabric. It is best to attach the material to the frame with a staple gun, rather than nails or tacks, as this minimises the amount of damage to the fabric.

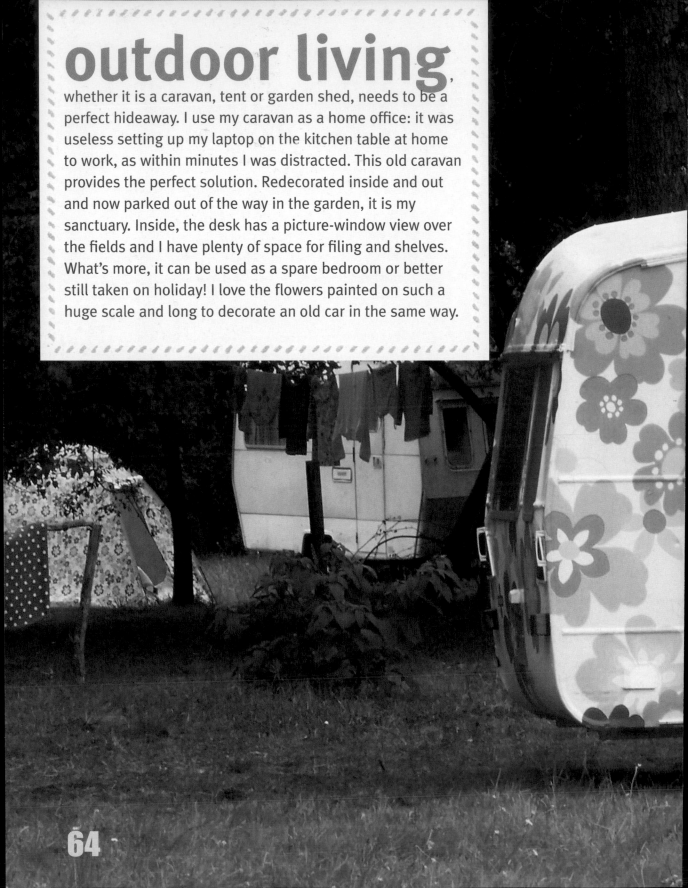

outdoor living,

whether it is a caravan, tent or garden shed, needs to be a perfect hideaway. I use my caravan as a home office: it was useless setting up my laptop on the kitchen table at home to work, as within minutes I was distracted. This old caravan provides the perfect solution. Redecorated inside and out and now parked out of the way in the garden, it is my sanctuary. Inside, the desk has a picture-window view over the fields and I have plenty of space for filing and shelves. What's more, it can be used as a spare bedroom or better still taken on holiday! I love the flowers painted on such a huge scale and long to decorate an old car in the same way.

doorstops

can be cheaply made by covering a standard builders' brick in a striking pop print. The brick does need some padding, such as curtain interlining, wrapped around it first to prevent it from chipping, but the fabric just needs to be stitched simply by hand (see page 158). I chose this seventies fabric as it has a rather cheeky, cartoon-like quality to it, but almost any print will work so long as it has a darkish ground, as the doorstep cannot be cleaned. They make great inexpensive presents; the weight only adds to the surprise once the doorstop is gift wrapped.

workboxes

and other fabric-covered boxes often turn up at antique markets. They are worth snapping up as they make excellent storage, particularly the ones with drawers and compartments. I now have a collection for my sewing kit, ribbons and buttons. All the clashing prints look great together on a shelf. If you can't find vintage boxes or want to use a particular print, simple shapes such as shoe boxes can be easily covered oneself.

tote bags work
well made from graphic seventies prints (see page 158). The antique metallic ribbon used for the handles contrasts against the abstracted florals. There are all sorts of ribbons around, from natural hessian to colourful stripes, that would work well as handles. They just need to be heavy enough so the handles don't curl.

mini florals

mini florals are some of the prettiest fabric prints. Although they are usually designed for clothing, they can be easily adapted for home furnishings. It is still possible to buy fabulous vintage designs – rolls of old shirting and lingerie prints do sometimes turn up at antique fairs – but there are also some great new designs on the market. The London department store Liberty's is famed for its floral prints, but most dressmaking shops have a good selection of old-fashioned floral prints.

Delicate, tiny florals are ideal for either making or trimming bedlinen. These small-scale prints are often found on very fine cotton, which is perfect for bedding. When trimming pillowcases, I tend to make two mis-matching pairs. I put four pillows on a bed, with each pair trimmed in a slightly different way.

Combine these small florals with other prints, such as classic gingham. I have made cushions from tiny floral prints, that I have teamed with a gingham check backing. Likewise, I have teamed a pair of gingham check curtains with a floral fabric pelmet. Other prints on a similar small scale, such as baby polka dots and classic shirt stripes, are also good foils for mini florals.

Strips of mini florals, cut on the cross as bias binding, makes a great trim or piping that can be applied to cushions or wool blankets. It also looks great around the hem of a skirt. Leave the edges of the piping frayed for a really vintage look, or even layer two prints on top of each other.

Second-hand shops often yield some of the best prints in the form of old shirts, aprons and housecoats. As these garments are often awful shapes, you don't need to feel guilty about chopping them up. The beaded necklace shown in this chapter was made from an old housecoat. The small scale of these designs make them ideal for tiny items such as little purses, coat hangers, and lavender bags. I had fun covering an old pair of shoe trees but pretty much anything works in these kind of prints.

Basic sewing projects are all I can manage, but I have advertised in my local newsagent for a dressmaker with great success. I am hopeless at following a pattern or copying other garments, but when I have known exactly want I wanted and given clear instructions, the results have been great. There are some exquisite printed silks around, which are ideal for clothing, so it may be worth trying to sew some simple shapes.

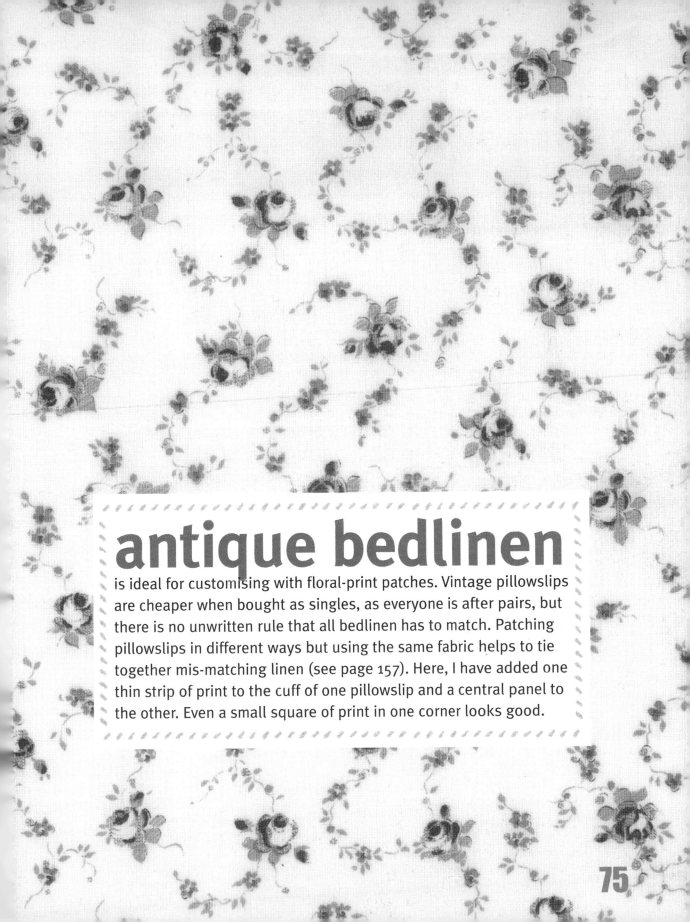

antique bedlinen

is ideal for customising with floral-print patches. Vintage pillowslips are cheaper when bought as singles, as everyone is after pairs, but there is no unwritten rule that all bedlinen has to match. Patching pillowslips in different ways but using the same fabric helps to tie together mis-matching linen (see page 157). Here, I have added one thin strip of print to the cuff of one pillowslip and a central panel to the other. Even a small square of print in one corner looks good.

frilled curtains

are the perfect partner for a short fabric pelmet. This style of window treatment has been out of fashion for a while, so pelmets are incredibly cheap to buy nowdays. I love the look of them, however, so when I found this old fashioned chintz pelmet minus its curtains, I made a pair in a basic red gingham (see page 158). I have left the curtains unlined as I love the way the light shines through the fabric, although I have also hung a plain white rollerblind with blackout lining at the window to block out the light in the morning. The simple gathered frills that edge the curtains echo the gentle gathers of the pelmet, which unifies the look despite the different prints.

zip-up purses

zip-up purses, when made with an extra waterproof lining, make excellent cosmetic bags. These Eastern European prints are traditionally red and white or blue and white toile, but any scraps of faded florals will look great together. You could even mix two different mini-floral prints within one purse.

handmade gifts

have a special quality to them. There are endless simple products to make from scraps of old fabric. Traditional items, like lavender bags, are always popular, but it is fun to think up something unusual. It can be easier to customise an existing product rather than start from scratch. Here, I have covered some old shoe trees to give as a gift along with a pair of my own design slippers (see page 158). The challenge is to always come up with something new!

ironing

on a table is a luxury, providing you have the space. My grandmother had a big old washroom and always had an ironing table out instead of a board. The secret is to heavily pad the tabletop with interlining or an old blanket and then cover it with cotton using a staple gun (see page 158). It is best to use a heavyweight cotton, as any fine fabric will wear out quite quickly. The prettier the print, the better, anything to cheer up such a dreary job!

silky camisoles,

like the one shown here, can be made up from lengths of old printed silk, which are quite easy to find. Silk is perfect for making into clothing, but as I can't follow a dressmaking pattern, I have to pay someone to sew things for me! Local newspapers are the ideal place to look for a dressmaker, or it is worth putting an advertisement in your local newsagents window. The easiest method is to trace the shape of the pieces from a favourite garment and keep it as simple as possible (see page 158).

simple
bags

, such as this envelope shape, are just right for holding jewellery. It is relatively easy to make, as it doesn't require a fastener; it just needs to be deep enough so you can fold over the top flap. Children's dress cottons are usually an ideal scale of print for this sort of small bag. The same shape will also work as an evening clutch bag, but you will need to use a stiff brocade or cotton so it is firm enough to hold its shape.

beads

beads covered with tiny scraps of fabric can create some fantastically bold jewellery. I found this mini-floral print on an old cleaning overall and knew it was the perfect all-over design to cover some wooden beads (see page 158). I love the eccentric mix of the floral print, plastic and metal beads threaded together to make this necklace. This fabric would also have made a great corsage or hair tie.

rubber gloves

are synonymous with the most boring household chores, yet they are an essential item. I like to customise this type of basic utility product (see page 158). Decorated with a brilliant yellow floral, these gloves bring a smile to my face whenever I see them dangling over the taps in our washroom!

pictoral prints are always included

in my collection of vintage fabrics. I so admire the skill of the designers; their draughtsmanship is often incredible, but it is the eccentricity of some of these retro designs that appeals to me. It is something that you rarely see in fabric prints today.

American prints are some of the best I have come across. Apart from classic cowboy designs, which inspired me when I first began to make my own designs, I have found fabrics with subject matter ranging from spacemen to beauty parlours. I have also found some great designs in the UK; these tend to appear at car boot sales and on internet auction sites. Very occasionally old rolls of pictoral wallpaper turn up too, which are worth snapping up as they are increasingly hard to find and even a single panel on a wall can look good.

Children's rooms are often where these prints work best. A pictoral print fabric laid under a glass tabletop is ideal as a bedside table. Some prints can frame up well into pictures. A lot of these designs are scenic and you can cut a number of different images from one print to make a great set of pictures. You can even do this by cutting up cheap polycotton bedlinen sets emblazoned with cartoon characters which are on sale all over the place.

Cushions are similarly an ideal use for this kind of print. With old fabrics there is usually not much to go around so I use a plain backing which also helps to set off the print. Children's fabrics are good for beanbags or floor cushions and corduroy makes a practical choice to go with them. If you don't have much material you can just put a square of the design as a centre piece on a larger cushion.

Obvious uses for specific prints often speak for themselves: great dog print simply had to be made into a pet bed for my terrier, Stanley. Other prints can be harder to place, but are worth buying and holding on to if they are a great design. A few years ago, I bought some spaceman fabric that I absolutely love, but I just couldn't make up my mind how to use it. It was only when I was redecorating my husband's office that I found its perfect home as the upholstery on his desk chair.

cushions

for kids' rooms are the perfect place to have a little fun. There are some superb pictoral fabrics around that are just right for basic cushions (see page 159). I love this French farmyard scene, particularly the cute sheep in the corner, but I had only a small piece. Taking one of my favourite sections, I hemmed the print into a square and applied the fabric panel to a polka dot cushion. Spot prints are a quintessential fabric for children's rooms as they have an enduring, uplifting quality to them.

tabletops

of plain glass placed over prints frame and protect the fabric. This cowboy print is preserved under glass as the top of a homework table. It is the perfect place to tuck in favourite photographs, which we add to over time. Bamboo bedsidetables and bathroom storage often paint up well and are ideal for taking a glass top; check they are not too wobbly before buying.

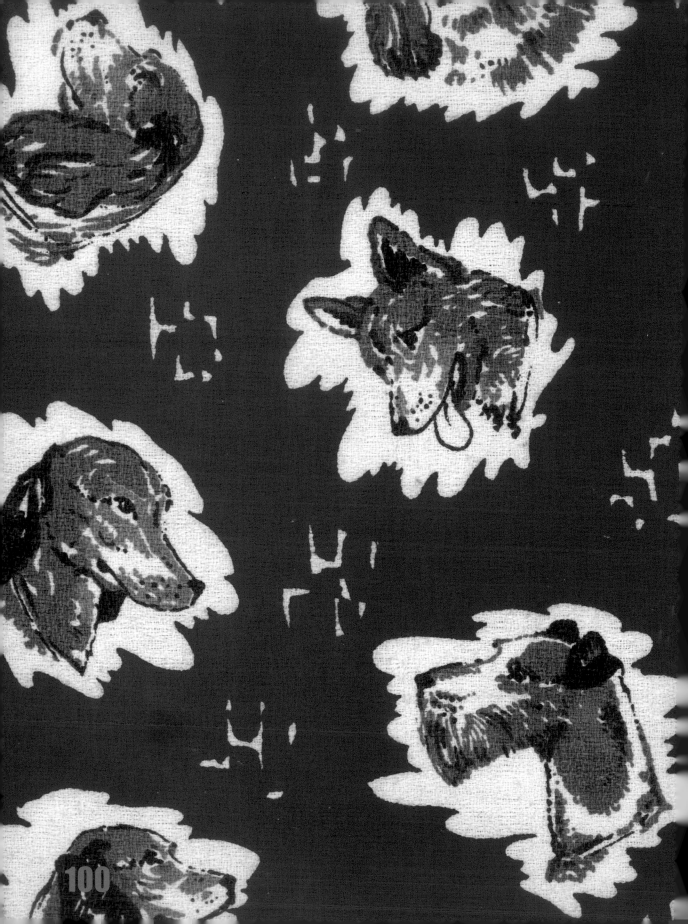

pet beds

take a lot of wear and tear, so they need frequent laundering. The bed on which my terrier, Stanley, sleeps is a large square cushion, so it is really simple to make a slip cover to fit – so simple, in fact, that Stanley has a choice of covers in prints ranging from old roses to polka dots (see page 157). I couldn't resist making an extra cover from this dog print fabric. He seems to like it, too.

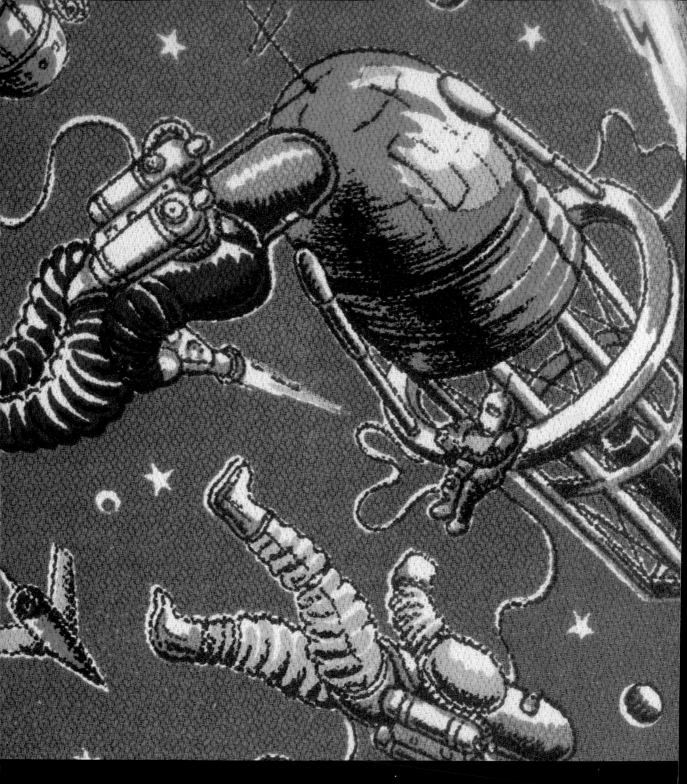

office chairs and children's pictoral
prints may seem an unlikely pairing, but, for me, this fabulous spaceman

print is the perfect upholstery fabric for an otherwise serious room.
I was lucky enough to find a whole curtain, so there was sufficient fabric to
have this chair professionally re-covered for a look that is out of this world!

cushion covers

are quick to make and so can be easily changed to give a room a different look – this is particularly useful in a child's room as you can change their bedroom subtly as their tastes grow up. All too often, kids want something new, which is why I reckon it is best to keep more expensive items, like curtains, plain. This boat print seemed to me ideal for a child's room, so I made it into basic cushions (see page 157). I have kept the style simple, without any fancy piping or trims, so that the nautical print, complemented by the polka dot backing fabric, is not detracted from.

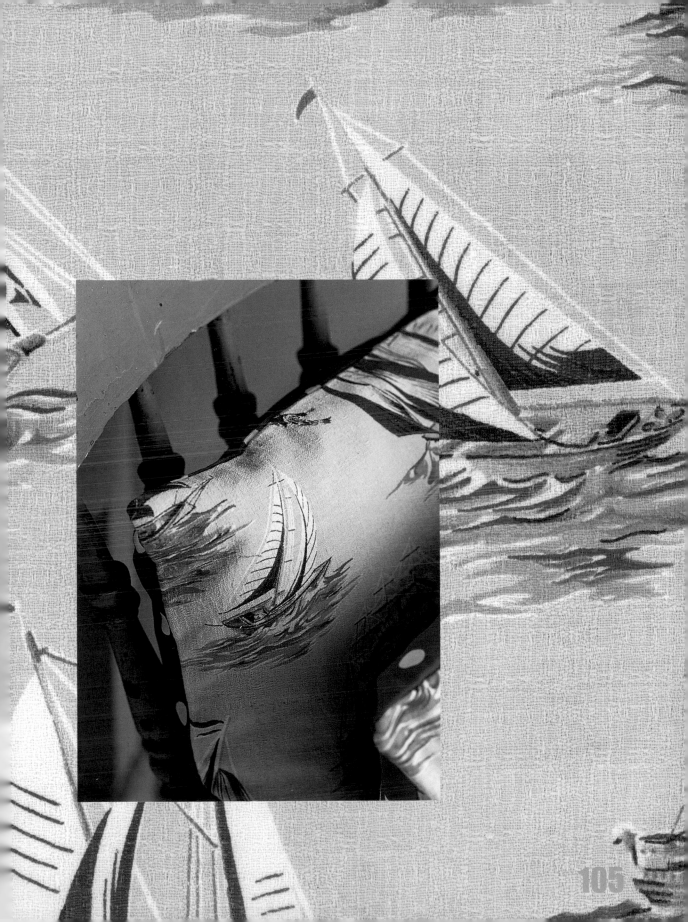

framed fabrics

can be a good way of showing off either small scraps of a favourite print or a precious vintage piece that you don't want to cut up. This sweet toile was ideal for cutting up into pictures, as each scene could be framed separately. The same can be done with cartoon-character fabrics, which are easy to buy as duvet covers. Even cheap modern ones work well when they are put into the right frames.

107

keyrings are an easy

project for children to make, particularly if you
cover over an existing fob. If an adult cuts the
material to size, then all the children have to do
is stick it over the fob and tack around the edges
with simple running stitches (see page 159).
This tiny scrap of horse fabric seemed ideal for
my pony-obsessed god daughter to use.

patchwork

patchwork is often considered as a means of repairing something that is past its best – patching it up. A friend, who was a textile dealer, sold highly fragile antique fabrics. Rather than apologising for the fact that they were repaired, she always raved about the patches on the materials she sold. Her passion for patches made me realise that patchwork can be an art form in its own right.

Worn-out chair seats and arms can be successfully repaired using patches. Recently, I needed to rescue an old armchair that was threadbare in places, but the original cover was really quite special. Rather than re-covering the entire chair or trying to match the original print, I patched it with another contrasting floral fabric. I then made an extra scatter cushion in the new print to complete the patchwork effect with delightful results. I have since repaired an eiderdown and cushions in the same way using a contrasting printed fabric.

Patchwork quilts I find irresistible. For years they have been a minimalist's nightmare, conjuring up visions of twee country cottages. But, it is all about how they are used: they look best in fairly plain rooms. They are ideal for throwing over the backs of chairs or sofas to cheer up a bland room. Whilst I like the classic faded sprig prints patchworks tend to to come in, there are some terrific bright coloured ones available. I have vintage patchworks from India in clashing hot pinks and oranges that have totally transformed my sitting room.

Layering prints, much like patching fabrics, runs the risk of looking too cluttered when lots of busy prints are put together. Again, it helps when the room itself is quite plain. I have layered up a couple of tablecloths on a big kitchen table which worked well and I love the piles of clashing printed notebooks on my desk where there are no other patterns around.

Combining lots of different prints to make your own patchwork projects is easy. I recently bought some great girls' dresses made from bordered tablecloths that had been sewn together with the borders forming stripes. This idea would work equally well for cushions. Strips of print can be added to ready-made plain items from skirts to pillows. Often they look good when the colours clash. The fun is to take random colours and patterns and throw them all together as if by accident!

gift wrap

can be easily made from your favourite fabric prints with just a basic scanner and printer attached to your computer. Simply scan a piece of fabric in and print it out on paper! If you have a basic knowledge of computers, it is relatively straightforward to change the colours or alter the scale of the design. I often print out large sheets of print on my industrial printer at work, but even regular A4-size sheets are useful in an emergency

114

patches

add character, especially when sewn on by hand (see page 157). I just love the delphinium print covering this chair, so I rescued it by making good the threadbare arms and seat with patches of another bold print. Hand stitch the patch in place as carefully or as roughly as you like. Here, adding a cushion in the same fabric as the patches brought it all together, making a feature of the two striking prints.

patchwork quilts

are really coming back into fashion and make perfect throws for armchairs and sofas. They are cheap to pick up when they are damaged, but they are then ideal for cutting up into cushions (see page 157) or to throw over a sofa where any blemishes will not to noticed. Traditional gingham and shirting stripes are usually a good choice for mixing in with floral patchworks or using as backing fabrics for cushions where extra is needed.

layering

these two tablecloths was really a happy accident – a single cloth on its own wasn't long enough to cover my kitchen table, so I used two. I was delighted with the effect. You could add to the mix-and-match vibe by using napkins in the same fabric as the underneath cloth.

kids' dresses

made from recycled tablecloths are such a neat idea.
I found this selection on a stall at Portobello Road, a
regular street market in West London. The print and
the colours are so much better than any new fabrics
available. There are some good basic patterns for
children's clothing: something like a simple A-line
skirt (see page 159) is easy to make if you have
never attempted any dressmaking before.

notebooks

covered in patterned papers are a habit picked up at school, which I just can't shake off. One of the highlights of my school holiday, before the new term started, was visiting the local stationers to stock up on books and papers. All these patterned papers were bought in a small village in Italy, where the shop owner still kept stock from thirty years ago. I particularly like the rasta-coloured paper juxtaposing the garden roses.

books, books, books

faded florals

faded florals gain in character as they age. Even the most worn-out print can have a use. Although it was disintegrating, I recently bought a huge piece of fabric simply for the inspiration I gleaned from its muted colour palette. It was very fragile and full of holes, but a friend suggested using it to line a laundry cupboard. It suited that use perfectly, and once it was stuck up with a fine layer of photographic spraymount, the holes only added to its crumbling character. I have also made lengths of delicate fabrics into panels and screens, which is an ideal use for fragile pieces. And if something is really damaged, it can always be patched with another similar fabric, which can add to its character.

Washed-out, pale colours are restful in a bedroom. There is nothing quite like a faded floral chair cover or eiderdown, but it is hard to find new fabrics that have the same antique appeal. It is best to avoid those fabrics with a fake vintage effect. You can achieve this look with modern fabrics: if you have the patience, leave your fabric out on the washing line over summer. After a period of time – depending on how strong the sun is – it will fade naturally. Although there is nothing like natural sunlight to do the trick, you can gradually bleach fabrics on a hot wash with some biological powder. However, it does take quite a few goes to achieve a proper washed-out look.

Staining fabrics with tea is another useful trick; natural fabrics, such as cottons, linens and wool blends, work best for tea dying. Fill a washing-up bowl with hot brewed tea, remove the tea bags, and submerge the fabric. Stir the contents of the bowl continuously with a wooden spoon or the fabric will stain unevenly and look blotchy. Once the fabric has soaked and is the colour you want, remove it from the bowl and rinse it through well with plenty of warm water and a little mild washing-up liquid. Alternatively, you can run a pale fabric dye through larger lengths of material in the washing machine. It is best to start with a very weak solution and build up the colour with a second wash, if necessary.

Pastel shades are pretty, too, and can be cleaner than some faded florals. To freshen up a bathroom, try combining pale turquoise with pink or washed lime with canary yellow in funky floral prints; great for a young girl's bedroom.

antique lace

in silver silk added to both ends of a length of floral muslin made a perfectly pretty shawl to wear to a party. The minimum sewing was needed, but the effect makes quite a statement. Muslin is an excellent handkerchief or scarf fabric, and very easy to hand sew. Long thin scarves are useful as they double up as a belts to wear with jeans.

lined cupboards

are exactly the sort of 'hidden extras' that I'm all in favour of. For me, it turns an otherwise mundane domestic chore, like putting away the laundry, into a secret pleasure. The material I used to line this linen cupboard was terribly old and frail, but it doesn't matter; the holes and fading add to its character. I used photographer's spraymount to cover the cupboard interior and pasted up the fabric, working quickly before the spray glue dried. Originally an uninspiring basic pine interior, the cupboard was transformed by the fabric lining.

customised clothing

has a unique appeal; it is a one-off. The patches added to this cardigan, on the elbows and front, serve a dual purpose: to give decorative interest to an otherwise plain garment and save darning any worn elbows. I find it easier to sew on patches than darn wool, so I add them to woollens, t-shirts and denims (see page 157).

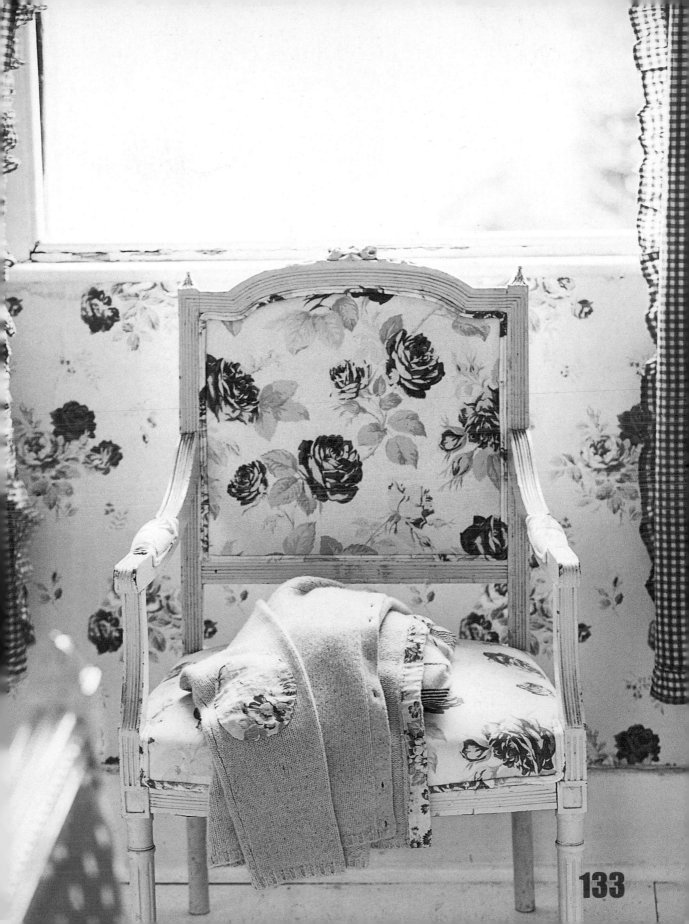

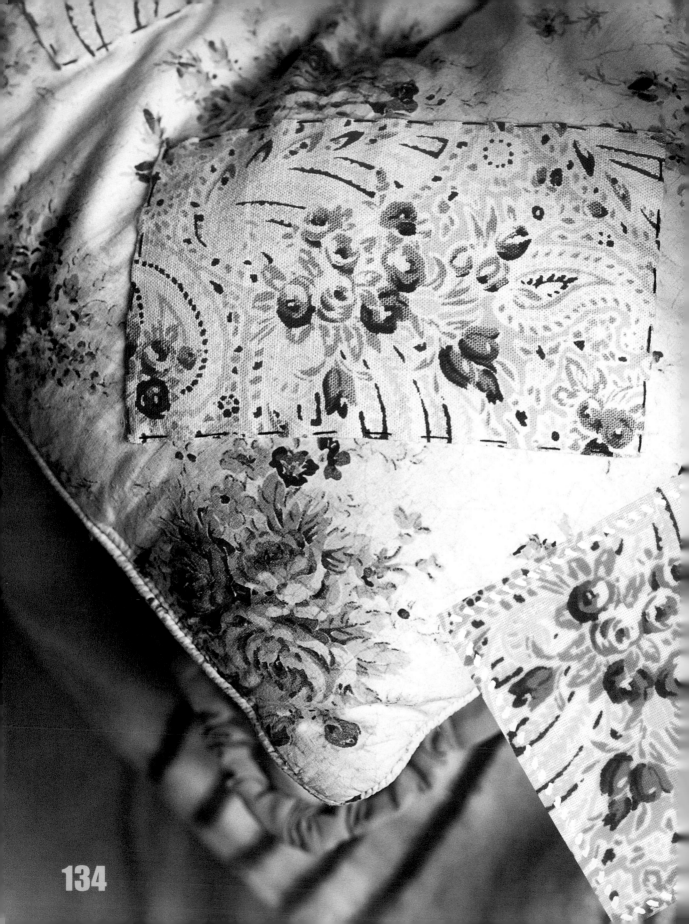

feather eiderdowns

are the cosiest thing, but they are becoming increasingly hard to find and often need repairing. This one was leaking feathers, but rather than try to disguise the holes, I patched it up in a really obvious way. Each patch was sewn on using a contrasting coloured thread, so the fabric squares form a pattern of their own (see page 157). I chose this fabric as it wasn't too dominant when layered on top of the original eiderdown, but you could go for a clashing contrast.

placemats

and napkins couldn't be simpler to make (see page 158). I prefer to hand sew them, as the uneven stitching has more character. They can be made from odd scraps of material. You don't have to make a matching set, you just need to choose prints of a similar character. Don't forget to put some cork, wicker or a heatproof mat underneath, if you need to protect your tabletop.

wall hangings can

breathe new life into fabrics, particularly large-scale prints that often take on a completely different character once framed (see page 158). There are some wonderful 'Tree of Life' designs around that tend to look rather old-fashioned as upholstery but look much better when used flat, either within a blind or as a decorative panel. It is worth looking out for old Indian cotton bedspreads with this sort of print as they make perfect panels to hang above a bed in place of a bedhead.

painterly florals

with a true hand-drawn quality are just magical, so it is worth considering how to use them to their best advantage. Some of my favourite painterly prints are surface-printed and hand-blocked wallpapers, to which the colour is applied by hand. There are companies that still use these methods to print wallpapers; although they are expensive, they are real works of art. If you are commissioning a short run of wallpaper you can choose your own colours. I am about to decorate my bathroom using a hand-printed paper. It is a large, airy room with plain white cupboards and bathroom fittings, and a shiny white linoleum floor, so the only decoration will be a bright rose-covered paper.

Examples of vintage wallpapers sometimes crop up. Snap them up to use as wonderful drawer linings or even as a single panel on a wall. If it is a big print, it can really dominate a room.

Treasured lengths of material are best suited to making into cushions, as you tend to take a pattern in at a relatively close distance. Make them up simply, with, at most, a simple braid or bobble fringe, and set them against a plain chair or sofa cover. Very bright, colourful prints of this kind are great outdoors and excellent for garden furniture. If you are lucky, you can sometimes come across old parasols with this sort of design.

Show off a particular favourite print by making it into a tote bag; I guarantee it will get a lot of use and be much admired. I have a couple of bags made from classic rose prints, and they are the one thing people always stop and ask me about. Some of the best painterly prints can be found on old fifties sundresses and summer skirts. For me, the problem is that they never fit because they all have such tiny waists, so chop them up. Although a really pretty party dress will look great left out on display, just hanging on the back of a door.

Bright colour combinations used in many vintage prints often surprise me. Some of the classic fifties florals are in outrageous colourways: clashing oranges and pinks with accents of black. When used sparingly, they can add that special element of surprise to a room.

shopper bags

are classic, especially when made up in an irresistible vintage print. They are very simple to sew, but are best made of a sturdy fabric (see page 158). The more they are washed, the better they become, as they seem to mellow with age. Old furnishing prints, that would look gloomy on a sofa, work really well when converted into a bag.

143

colourful cottons

combined with cheap wool fringing gives a cushion a lovely summery feel (see page 157). I use this cushion, made from an old sundress, outdoors on a painted cane chair. As is often the case, this sort of fringing looks better once it has been washed.

pretty boxes

and old cake tins are always worth collecting. I use them to package up gifts, such as homemade cakes. I lined this beautiful cardboard box with crisp pink tissue paper and filled it with chocolates, but an old-fashioned tin with an iced sponge cake inside always goes down well. I cheat by buying cakes at my local farmers' market, but I have given up pretending I make them myself as, more often than not, I get caught out!

148

flower prints

make the most fabulous cushions and often need just the plainest of backings. This exquisite dahlia print looks better without the print on the back, so I have used a basic white linen to make up these cushions. I have added a white bobble fringe for a bit more character (see page 157). You can still buy crocheted cotton lace in dressmaking shops, which is good alternative trim.

where to shop

antique fairs and markets
Search for the details of local antique fairs, markets and auctions in a magazine called *Antiques Trade Gazette*, who also have an online search facility on their website, www.antiquestradegazette.com. Vintage clothing fairs are good places to hunt for fabrics, as they are often attended by textile dealers. Well-known markets, such as Portobello Road in West London and Camden Passage in North London, can be expensive, but they are still worth checking out. The best fairs are held outdoors, usually early in the morning at venues like racecourses, agricultural showgrounds and old airfields.

house clearance and charity shops
This is where you can find real bargains. They usually have an area dedicated to textiles, so it is easy to dash in and out during your lunch hour. If you find nothing at first, don't be put off. Stock changes pretty quickly in charity shops and is unpredictable, so when you do come across something, it is all the more satisfying. I appreciate the recycling aspect of shopping for second-hand fabrics, and if the money is going to charity, that is an added bonus.

151

car boot sales
For me, a good car boot sale is the best fun. When I'm at home in Gloucestershire, I go every Sunday morning, making it back in time for breakfast laden with treasures. You just never know what you will find. For textiles, you often have to rifle through piles of old clothes, which can be off-putting, however, you can find some amazing fabrics that simply don't come up at antique markets at great prices. Find out where your local car boot sales are held by visiting www.carbootcalendar.com.

street markets
Whenever I am abroad, I always check out the local street market. The stalls to look out for are those selling bed linen and towelling, dressmaking fabrics and kitchen wares. I have bought pillowcases, tablecloths, yards of great printed fabrics and drawer lining papers, for example. It is also worth visiting local markets at home. They can be an excellent source for basic fabrics, like gingham.

hardware stores and haberdashery shops
These shops are increasingly scarce, but they are often an Aladdin's cave. Hardware stores are a great source for sticky-back plastic and oilcloth, but look for old-fashioned tea towels, placemats and napkins, too. Haberdashery shops often have bolts of vintage materials, so it is worth asking whether they have old stock tucked away. There are many more of these types of stores in Europe and further afield. I have just been in Morocco and the sewing shops there had an amazing range of fabrics. It is best to find the areas where the locals shop, rather than visiting the tourist markets.

local newspapers
Check out your local newspaper for charity sales and fêtes. There are nearly always great bric-a-brac stalls at these events. I have bought good ready-made items, such as covered coat hangers, homemade jam with fabric lids and fragrant lavender bags. There are always great homemade cakes, if nothing else! Local newspapers are also a good place to find the details of dressmakers and upholsterers. In the past, I have placed advertisements in my local newsagent's window and found excellent sewing help this way.

internet auction sites

The internet really has changed the way we shop. Browsing an internet auction site, such as www.ebay.com, is now one of the easiest ways to track down vintage fabrics. I have discovered if I tap my own name into an eBay search, a mass of floral prints comes up with the description ' very Cath Kidston'. It has been quite a challenge to buy items under a pseudonym. You do have to be really careful when buying fabrics sight unseen. So much stuff looks good online, but quite a lot of it isn't original – simply 'vintage style' – and actually quite expensive for what it is. It is always worth asking the fabric content and checking the condition things are in before placing a bid.

online shopping

Like many retailers, I offer a mail order service through my website. My own design fabrics and products are available to buy online, just click on www.cathkidston.co.uk.

tips for successful shopping

- Always go on the first day of a two-day fair. Not only do most of the best things go first, but a lot of dealers leave before the second day. The 'Trade' entrance fee will cost more, but it is worth it.
- Ask for a trade discount. Most dealers will automatically offer about 10% off, you just have to ask!
- If you go to an early morning fair, do take a torch! It can be absolutely pitch dark when they open, especially in winter, and the best bargains are to be had when people are unpacking.
- Take lots of small change and fivers. People are always short and often accept a deal if you proffer the right money.
- It can often be cold even in the summer. Fingerless gloves are a must in the winter so you can pick things up without taking your gloves off!
- Always unfold and examine textiles. Dealers can be ruthless in hiding holes and stains.

sewing tips

making your own pattern Whether you are sewing a loose cover for a chair or copying a favourite camisole top, create the pattern pieces by pinning sheets of newspaper to each section of the item and draw around the shape to be cut out. Remember to add extra for the seam allowance all the way around each piece.

preparing your fabric Before cutting, wash your fabric at the specified temperature then run an iron over it; this makes cutting easier and more accurate.

pinning out pieces When laying out all the pattern pieces on your fabric, follow the straight grain, unless they are to be cut on the bias. If your fabric has a bold print, such as a check or stripe, line up the pieces so patterns will match up.

cutting out pieces When cutting out your fabric, cut carefully around each paper pattern piece.

joining pieces Pin and tack the pieces of fabric together before stitching the seams. Remove all the pins before sewing.

pressing pieces Before continuing your sewing, press each seam, hem and dart. Place your iron and ironing board or table nearby when you are ready to begin stitching. Test a scrap of your fabric for pressing before you begin to sew. Each seam, no matter how short, should be pressed as soon as it is stitched. Then the piece which will be joined to it will lie flat.

neatening threads Neaten your sewing by snipping off all stray threads.

sewing techniques

running stitches Running stitches can be used for seams that do not receive much strain. Secure the thread at one end with a knot or two tiny backstitches. Pass the needle through the fabric, taking up the small possible amount for each stitch, making sure they are evenly spaced along the length of the fabric. Finish with two backstitches to fasten.

tacking stitches Use long running stitches to hold the fabric in position for final stitching. Start with a knot and leave unfastened at the end. To remove tacking stitches, clip the thread at intervals before pulling out the stitches. Pulling too long a thread can mar the fabric. When tacking delicate fabrics like silk, use a fine thread that won't mark the cloth.

back stitches Fasten the thread and make a running stitch. Now take a stitch back, placing the needle in the work at the beginning of the first stitch and bring it out a stitch ahead. Continue in this way.

simple seams Zig-zag stitch along any raw edges to neaten, either before or after joining the seams. Pin and then tack the right sides of the fabrics together. Remove the pins and machine-stitch. Remove the tacking and press the seam open.

plain hems Turn the hem to the wrong side to the required depth, press and stitch. Alternatively, turn 1cm to the wrong side and press. Then turn the hem over again to the required depth and pin or tack. Press. Stitch hem close to the first fold.

hand-stitched hems Fasten the thread under the fold of the hem; take a tiny stitch, catching a thread or two of the fabric under the fold and bring the needle through the edge of the fold. The stitches should be small and even and slightly slanted.

oversew stitches Hold the edges to be sewn together. Take the stitches over the edge with the needle held in a slanted position.

gathers Leaving a long loose thread-end at the beginning, work running stitches along the length of the fabric and secure the end with backstitches. Then slide the fabric along the thread until it is evenly gathered. Secure the loose thread-end by twisting in a figure of eight around a pin. Adjust the gathering as required. If attaching a gathered frill, pin or tack the frill to the right side of the fabric and stitch. Topstitch along the right side of the fabric, close to the seam, to neaten.

ties Fold the fabric in half lengthways with right sides together and pin or tack. Stitch around two sides leaving one end open for turning. Trim the corner. Turn right side out. The blunt end of a pencil may be used for pushing the ends through. Fold inside the raw edges of the open end of the ties for neatness before attaching. For pointed ends, stitch and cut at an angle of 45 degrees.

darts To shape an item, such as the bean bags on page 12, stitch a dart. With right sides of the fabric together, mark your v-shaped dart with a ruler and chalk. Fold the fabric between the marking in a straight line to form a point. Pin. Tack the dart from the point to the widest part. Stitch the dart from the widest part to the point. If the dart is more than 1.5cm deep, slash and press open. Otherwise press darts downwards.

bias binding Cut strips of fabric across the bias (on a diagonal fold). Lap the strips so the thread of the fabric is parallel and seam where the edges meet. Stitch the strips together to form long lengths. Fold and press the edges to the centre of the strip, ready to attach the binding. Trim any extending corners. Stitch the binding strip and fabric along the hem edge with right sides together. Turn the binding over the hem edge; turn under the raw edge of the binding strip and hem to the machine stitching on the inside.

reinforced stitching Attach a tie, loop or handle by stitching the ends with a square. Then stitch across the square on both diagonals. Repeat for an extra-secure finish.

piped seams Cover a length of piping cord with a strip of bias binding and stitch close to the cord, using a sewing machine with a piping or zipper foot attachment. Place the covered piping cord between the seam edges with finished edge extending beyond the seam line and all the raw edges together. Pin, then tack in place. Stitch on the inside, again using the correct foot attachment, close to the piping.

neat corners To make a neat point at a corner, turn the edges in and crease. Fold the point in, diagonally across the corner where the creases meet. In bulky, heavy fabrics, the corner should be trimmed away. Turn on creased lines and tack folded edges. Press.

overlapping corners Mark the width of the hem and trim the fabric where the hem overlaps to within a seam's width of the edge. Turn and tack. Hem the turned edges down and slip-stitch lower edges together.

patch pockets Turn in the seam allowance at the top of the pocket. Turn a hem at the top to the outside and stitch ends. Turn and press side seams in. Turn hem to inside enclosing seams. Slip-stitch. Turn up point at bottom of pocket. Turn and press remainder of the seams along the pointed bottom edge. Tack pocket on garment and top-stitch close to edge, pivoting at corners. For curved pockets, clip at the curves so the pocket will lie flat.

project instructions

bean bag (see page 10) When using an existing bean bag as a template, trace the pieces onto your fabric, adding 1.5cm seam allowance. When starting from scratch, cut two circles of fabric to desired size, adding 1.5cm seam allowance. Measure the circumference of this circle and cut a side panel to this measurement by the height required, again adding 1.5cm seam allowance. Join the ends of the side panel by sewing a simple seam (see page 154). Lay one circle of fabric right side up and place the side panel over the top, right side down, aligning the raw edges. Pin and tack. Sew with a 1.5cm simple seam. To attach the bottom circle, lay it right side up and align the remaining raw edges of the side panel, right sides down, around the perimeter. Pin, tack and then stitch together, leaving a gap to insert the filling. Turn right side out. Fill with polystyrene beads and close the opening using small, neat oversew stitches (see page 155).

upholstered chair cushion (see page 14) Trace the contours of the cushion top to make the pattern pieces and transfer onto your fabric, adding 1.5cm seam allowance. Cut out. Using a plain fabric for the underside, cut out another piece the same size. Measure the perimeter of the top panel and cut a side panel to this measurement by the height required, adding 1.5cm seam allowance. Join this strip into a band with a simple seam (see page 154). If you have enough fabric, make strips of bias binding to cover a length of piping cord (see page 155). Lay the top panel right side up and cut a piece of covered piping cord to the perimeter of the panel. With raw edges aligning, pin and tack the piping to the outside edge. With right sides facing and starting at the centre back, pin the side panel to the top panel, taking care to pin it right into the corners. Stitch with 1.5cm seams. If necessary, clip the seam allowance at the corners to ease the seams. Attach the bottom panel to the side panel in the same manner, leaving an opening for the cushion. Turn right side out. Insert the cushion. Close the opening using small, neat oversew stitches.

appliqué patches (see page 16, 74, 116, 132 and 134) Cut a piece of fabric to the size of patch required, adding a 1cm hem allowance to each edge. Turn a 1cm plain hem (see page 154) to the wrong side of each edge, taking care at each corner, either folding them in to a neat point or overlapping them (see page 155). Handstitch the fabric patch to the item using small, neat running stitches (see page 154).

cook's apron (see page 18) Trace the pieces onto your fabric, making the bib (top) approximately two thirds the width of the skirt (bottom) and gently curving the sides of the bib out to meet the outside edges of the skirt, adding 1cm hem allowance. Cut out. Sew a 1cm plain hem (see page 154) along each edge, taking care when sewing around any curves. Cut out a length of fabric to make two ties (see page 155) for the waist and one tie for the neck strap. Add one tie to each edge of the apron at the waist, sewing with reinforced stitching where they join the upper outside edge of the skirt (see page 155). Stitch each end of the neck strap to the top edge of the bib, making sure that the strap does not twist. If preferred, finish by adding patch pockets to the skirt just below waist level (see page 155), taking care to match up the prints.

tablecloth, towel, tea towel and placemat (see pages 20, 46, 50, 120 and 136) Use the same method for each. Cut the fabric to the size required, adding 5cm hem allowance all the way around. Turn under both ends 2.5cm twice, press and tack. Turn in both sides in the same way, keeping the corners neat (see page 155). Stitch close to the edge of the folds. For a towel or a tea towel, to make a hanging loop, make a very thin tie (see page 155) or cut a length of ribbon. Fold in half and stitch ends together to make a loop. Sew the loop securely to one corner.

loose cover for bedhead (see page 26) Trace the contours of the bedhead to make the pattern pieces and transfer to your fabric, adding 1.5cm seam allowance. Cut out. Using a plain fabric for the back, trace and cut out another piece the same size. Measure the perimeter of the front panel, minus the bottom edge, and cut a side panel to this measurement by the depth required, adding 1.5cm seam allowance. If you have enough fabric, make strips of bias binding to cover a length of piping cord (see page 155). Lay the front panel right side up and cut a piece of the covered piping cord to the perimeter of the panel, minus the bottom edge. With raw edges aligning, pin and tack the piping to the outside edge. With right sides facing, pin the side panel to the front, taking care to pin it right into the corners. Stitch with 1.5cm seams. Clip the seam allowance around the corners to ease the seams. Attach the back to the side panel in the same manner, leaving the bottom edge open. Turn right side out. Sew a plain hem all the way around the bottom edge of the cover to finish (see page 154).

laundry bag (see page 28) Cut a piece of fabric to twice the required width of the bag by the height, adding 1.5cm seam allowance. With right sides together, fold the piece in half widthways. Pin and tack seams along bottom and side edges. Stitch along the bottom edge with 1.5cm seams (see page 154). Stitch the side seam, stopping 3.5cm short of the top edge. At the top edge, turn 1cm to the wrong side and press. Turn another 2.5cm hem and press. Pin and tack close to the edge of the folds along the hem to make the channel for the drawstring. Stitch. Thread a length of cord through this channel, or make a long tie (see page 155) to use instead of cord. To add an appliqué, cut out your preferred print, then pin and tack in place on the bag. Attach to the bag using small, neat oversew stitches (see page 155).

lampshade (see pages 32 and 56) Cut a length of fabric to the dimensions of the shade, adding 1cm hem allowance. Using non-flammable spray glue, stick the fabric to the shade, overlapping the ends and turning 1cm hems to the inside at top and bottom edges. Make sure the hems are not too deep as they will be visible when the lamp is on. For the frilled shade shown on page 32, make a gathered frill (see page 155) to fit the circumference of the shade and stitch around the bottom edge. Feather butterflies bought from habardashers can be held in place away from the lightbulb, with glue or a couple of small handstitches.

bedcover (see page 34) Cut your fabric to the size required, adding 5cm hem allowance. If necessary, join two or more widths of fabric with 5cm simple seams (see page 154) to achieve the size of bedcover required. Turn under both ends 2.5cm twice, press and tack. Turn in both sides in the same way, keeping the corners neat (see page 155). Stitch close to the edge of the folds.

upholstered steps or stool (see page 42) Cut a piece of oilcloth to the size of the top of the step or stool seat, adding enough extra on each edge to cover the sides of the step or seat and to turn to the underside. With the oilcloth in position, tack the fabric in place on the underside using a staple gun or upholstery nails and a hammer. Pay particular attention to the corners; fold them in neatly as you would when wrapping a parcel, trimming any excess where necessary.

wall hanging (see pages 60 and 138) To avoid cutting your fabric, buy a set of artists' stretcher strips that make a frame at least 10cm smaller than the material. Make up the frame by fitting together the mitred ends of each strip. Check the squareness of the frame by measuring across the corners, ensuring both measurements are equal. With the fabric right side down, position the frame centrally on top. Fold one edge of the fabric over the frame and tack in the centre using a staple gun, allowing 5cm excess. Move to the opposite side of the frame, pull the fabric firmly and tack with a staple in the centre. Move to an adjacent side and do the same, pulling firmly and tacking the fabric to the frame at the centre. Add a fourth tack on the opposite side. Moving out from the centre of each long side, pull the fabric taut and tack to the frame every 5cm, leaving about 5cm untacked at each corner. Repeat for the short sides. Pay attention to the corners; fold them in neatly as though wrapping a parcel. Tack the corners through the folded fabric while keeping it taut.

doorstop (see page 66)
Wrap a standard builder's brick in some protective padding, such as curtain interlining. Cut a piece of fabric large enough to wrap all the way around the padded brick, with enough on either edge to cover the sides, adding 1.5cm seam allowance. With the wrong side out, wrap the fabric around the brick, pinning it in place, tailoring the cover to fit snugly down all four corners but leaving an open flap on the bottom. Remove the cover from the brick and tack the pinned side seams. Stitch (see page 154). Trim excess seam allowance. Turn right side out and place the cover over the brick. Turn under 1cm hems on all three sides of open flap and slip stitch to the sides all the way around to close (see page 155).

tote bag (see pages 70 and 142)
Cut two pieces of fabric to the size of bag required, adding 1.5cm seam allowance. With right sides together, stitch simple seams (see page 154) along three sides, leaving the top edge open. Turn right side out. To make a lining, cut two pieces of lining fabric to the same size as the bag, adding 1cm seam allowance. With right sides together, stitch seams along three sides, leaving the top edge open. Turn 1cm hem to wrong side of open edge. Press. Turn 1.5cm hem to wrong side of open edge of bag. Pin and tack. For the handles, make two wide ties (see page 155) to the length required or cut two lengths of ribbon. Pin in position, one on each side of the bag, making sure they do not twist. Stitch down each edge of the handles, using reinforced stitching at the ends where necessary (see page 155). With wrong sides together, pin and tack the open edge of the lining to the inside top edge of the bag. Slip stitch the lining in place, sewing as close to the top edge of the bag as possible.

frilled curtains (see page 76)
For the curtains, cut two lengths of fabric to the drop required plus 17cm seam allowance. For the frills, cut two lengths of fabric to one and a half times the drop required by 10cm wide. Lay the fabric right side down and turn in both sides 1.25cm. Pin, tack and stitch. Turn down the top 2cm, press and oversew (see page 155) by hand. Lay a length of 5cm-wide curtain tape 0.5cm from the top, and turn under 1.25cm at either end. Pin, tack and stitch along all the edges of the tape. To make the frills, zigzag stitch around the perimeter of each strip. Turn in one long edge 0.5cm, press and stitch. Turn down both short edges 0.5cm, press and stitch. Handsew a running stitch along the unhemmed long edge and gather to the drop required (see page 155). Turn up the bottom of the curtain 7.5cm and press. Turn up another 7.5cm, press and stitch a plain hem by hand (see page 154). Lay the curtain right side down and pin the frill edging along the leading edge of the curtain so that only the frill part is exposed. Pin and tack in place. Turn the curtain right side up and machine down the leading edge to incorporate the frill.

zip-up purse (see page 78)
Cut two pieces of fabric to the size of purse required, adding 2.5cm seam allowance (in total, 5cm larger than zipper). Turn in 2.5cm along one long edge of each piece. Press. With zipper facing up, place folded edges of each piece along the outside edge of the closed zipper so that they almost meet in the middle. Pin and tack. Stitch. Open zipper. Fold the joined fabric pieces along zipper edge so they are right sides together. Stitch along other three edges with 2.5cm seams. Turn right side out.

shoe trees (see page 81)
Cut two circles of fabric to wrap around the toes, adding 1.5cm hem allowance. Turn and press 1.5cm hem around each circle. Handsew running stitches around edges of each circle. Place fabric circles over shoes trees, draw threads of running stitches to gather fabric around toes. When fabric is gathered tight, fasten off. Tie a length of ribbon into a bow around each shoe tree to disguise any joins.

ironing table (see page 82) Cut a piece of interlining or a blanket to the size of your tabletop, adding enough to fold over the sides and turn to the underside of the tabletop. Cut a piece of heavyweight cotton slightly larger than the size of the interlining. For securing the material to the table, follow the method given for stretching fabric over a frame to create a wall hanging, using either tacks and a hammer or a staple gun.

camisole top (see page 84) Using an existing camisole top as a template, trace all the pieces onto your fabric, adding 1.5cm seam allowance. Cut out piece and zigzag stitch all raw edges. If necessary, sew a dart (see page 155) in each side of front to shape. With right sides together, pin and tack front to back along side seams. Stitch with 1cm simple seams (see page 154). Make thin shoulder straps using method given to make ties (see page 155). Stitch each strap in place, on corresponding points of front and back. Turn right side out. With right sides together, pin and tack a lace trim around the top and bottom edges, as shown on page 85. Stitch with 1cm seams. Open out the seams and topstitch on the right side of silk close to the seam edge.

beaded necklace (see page 88) Cut small rectangles of fabric to size of each bead with a little extra. Apply a fabric glue to each bead and stick on fabric patch. Fold any excess fabric in at top and bottom of each bead; alternatively cut small v-shapes out of edges to minimise excess. Once glue is dry, string beads onto a length of cord or a thin fabric tie (see page 155) to make into a necklace or bracelet.

rubber gloves (see page 90) Cut a strip of fabric with pinking shears to three times the circumference of the glove cuff. Fold and press in pleats all along the length of the fabric strip. Cut the cuffs of the gloves with pinking shears. Turn the gloves wrong side out. Pin a pleated strip around each cuff. Stitch. Pin together the ends of the pleated strip where they meet to make a band. Stitch. Turn gloves right side out.

keyring (see page 108) Cut piece of fabric to size required to cover shop-bought keyfob, adding 1.cm seam allowance. With right sides out, stick the fabric to the keyfob using fabric glue. Using running stitches (see page 154), handsew around each edge. Trim any excess fabric to neaten.

cushion cover (see page 100, 118, 144 and 148) For the front panel, cut a piece of fabric to the size of the cushion pad adding 2cm seam allowance. For the back panels, cut a piece of fabric the same length but half the width of the cushion pad plus 3cm and adding 2cm seam allowance on other sides. Cut another piece of fabric half the width of the cushion pad plus 12cm and adding 2cm seam allowance on other sides. Lay the two back panels right sides down and turn in a double 1cm hem (see page 154) on one short side of each. Pin, tack and then stitch. Press. To add a trim: with the front panel right side up, lay the trim around the edges of the fabric so that it is 1cm in from the raw edges. Pin and tack. To add piping: with front panel right side up, lay the piping around the edges of the front panel so the raw edges of the panel and the selvedge of the piping are aligned and the piped side lies 1cm inside the cushion edge. With right sides together, lay the two back panels over the front panel with raw sides edge to edge so that the two seamed edges overlap by 9cm. Pin or tack pieces together 1cm from edges. Stitch with simple seams (see page 154). Turn right side out. Press. Insert cushion pad.

kid's clothing (see page 122) To make a simple A-line skirt, cut two pieces of fabric for front and back, making bottom edge of skirt approximately one third wider than the top edge. With right sides together, pin and tack pieces along sides. Stitch with 1cm simple seams (see page 154). Turn and press 2cm to wrong side twice around top edge. Pin and tack. Stitch, leaving a small opening at centre of front for threading through elastic. Attach end of length of 1cm-wide elastic to a safety pin and thread through waistband. Knot elastic together at when waist is required size. Trim any loose ends. Stitch across opening. Try on skirt and pin hem at required length. Turn, press and stitch plain hem (see page 154) at bottom edge of skirt where pinned.

acknowledgements All my thanks to: Pia Tryde and

Marco Sandemann, Andy Luckett and Kane Dowell, Jo-Ann Sanders, Karina Mamrowicz, Jennie and John Morgan, Elaine Ashton, Anne, Helen, Lisa and Claire at Quadrille, Hugh and Jess, and the entire team at 'Cath Kidston' who all have helped so much on this project.

Project Editor Anne Furniss
Creative Director Helen Lewis
Editor Lisa Pendreigh
Designer Claire Peters
Photographer Pia Tryde
Production Director Vincent Smith
Production Controller Ruth Deary

This edition first published in 2006 by Quadrille Publishing Ltd,
Alhambra House, 27–31 Charing Cross Road, London WC2H 0LS
Text and project designs © Cath Kidston, 2005
Photography © Pia Tryde, 2005
Design and layout © Quadrille Publishing Ltd, 2005

Cataloguing in Publication Data: a record for this book is available from the British Library.
ISBN-13: 978 1 84400 323 5
ISBN-10: 1 84400 323 X

Printed in China